Hidden No More

LATRICE CHENEE

WESTBOW
PRESS®
A DIVISION OF THOMAS NELSON
& ZONDERVAN

WestBow Press books may be ordered through booksellers or by contacting:

WestBow Press
A Division of Thomas Nelson & Zondervan
1663 Liberty Drive
Bloomington, IN 47403
www.westbowpress.com
844-714-3454

ISBN: 978-1-6642-9785-2 (sc)
ISBN: 978-1-6642-9787-6 (hc)
ISBN: 978-1-6642-9786-9 (e)

Library of Congress Control Number: 2023907001

Print information available on the last page.

WestBow Press rev. date: 04/27/2023

To my four amazing son shines: Reggie III, Reylen, Liam, and Thre3. Also, to my loves in heaven who are no longer with us: my mother, Pansy Louise; my father, LeRoy Donahue; and my two grandmothers, Sadie and Esther.

I used to say why me.

Why did you take my mother from me,

age 16, I had no understanding.

My father's attention stripped from me, his love

shown was substance afflicted, drug addiction.

Broken relationships, issues of abandonment.

Uncovered, people pleasing, choking on

my tears, strangled by my fears.

Lost, bound in mental prison surrounded by dream

killers, couldn't see my way out, blurred vision.

Depression and low self-esteem kept me in bondage

to what I thought I was missing, I thought it was my

reality, but it was an illusion, the adversary's fallacy.

Until I called on the name of Jesus and His love lifted

me, out of the things that tried to hold me, control

me, and then I began to let Christ mold me.

Cocooned in His love, He shows me my identity,

who I always was, who He created me to be.

His love overwhelming, this is my reality, on Him I

can depend, abide in, I never want to break free.

His love lifts me to a never experienced place of

intimacy, and I will follow Him for all eternity.

—LCW

CONTENTS

ACKNOWLEDGMENTS

The greatest achievement is an assist; we all need them. I love the quote from the State Farm commercial with Chris Paul: "A little assist goes a long way, no matter who it comes from." So I'd like to take this moment to share my gratitude with all those who assisted me during my most major transitions. My spiritual mother and father Apostle Helen Saddler and Bishop George Saddler, thank you for laboring for me and with me; for the strategic spirit-led calls to check in on me; for trusting God and giving me the responsibility of leadership at that appointed time; and for staying in His presence to get an on-time word from heaven for God's people, whether it was personal or corporate. Thank you for teaching and training us on how to have a personal relationship and for correcting us in love and pushing us into purpose. I am grateful, and I always say that I was well loved and favored by God, for He sent me to such a house as Into His Chambers Ministries International during the season I was in.

My spiritual mother Dr. Cheri Pavi Givens, you are my search and rescue in the spirit—my spiritual Harriet Tubman. Thank you for always praying for me, mentoring me, and interceding for me—most importantly during a very challenging time in my life. You are so amazing to me; I love the heart you have for your spiritual daughters and sons. Thank you for loving Jesus the way you do and for your intimacy and covenant with Him. Your worship ignited a desire and started a flame inside me. I'll never forget the night I met the King for real. Your obedience led me into His chambers, and my life has never been the same.

To all my iron sharpeners, including my sister cousins, my love for you all waives my dislike for some of our conversations. Thank you for the encouragement, the "get it all the way together" speeches, and the prayers from those who believed God's promises concerning my life. Thank you for helping me to safety when my wings were at their weakest points and I couldn't figure out how to fly. Thank you for being there when it hurt so badly and for wiping my tears and telling me to put my big girl panties on.

My grandparents are the real MVPs. May Sadie and Esther rest. Their support of me during my greatest time of adversity is what helped to sustain my sons and me. Thank you for planting the seed of Jesus Christ, for always ministering to me, and for praying for me daily. I am a product of Ephesians 6:4. I love you, Papa. May God continue to satisfy you with a long life.

To my girls—the ones who have been rocking with me for over thirty years and have been more to me and my sons than they will ever know—thank you for treating my sons like real nephews. Thank you for loving me through all my changes and development and for never judging me, even though you didn't always understand. Thank you for accepting me always and loving me unconditionally. Let us be an example, from pullovers and sneakers to Mac lipsticks and stiletto's and then back to sneakers. Cheers to the golden-girl years. It is a fact that women can keep healthy friendships.

To my aunty mom, Veronica Ybarra, you are always there when I need to know if something is spoiled, ask for new recipes, talk about what's new, or just an ear to listen. Thank you. Just as your concrete porch held me and my tears during the most intense prayer I've ever prayed while my mom was laying lifeless around the corner, you have been a concrete pillar of support to me. I love you.

I have several more, I am certain; however, it may be a book alone just to acknowledge everyone. Charge it to my head, not my heart. Thank you to all who support me in any way. It is greatly appreciated, and I am eternally grateful.

INTRODUCTION

It's a butterfly thing. After exploring the life of a butterfly, I learned that it was very detailed. God began to show me how my life had spiritual similarities to a butterfly's. The life cycle has four stages: egg, larva, pupa, and adult. Each stage has a different purpose that is necessary for development, much like us. A butterfly starts its life as an egg that is very small in size. All butterfly eggs are unique, and they vary based off what type of butterfly they will be. The eggs must be laid on plants that are growing in very precise conditions—just the right amount of shade and just the right temperature and humidity. This is crucial for development because the larvae of most species will only eat the leaves of one or two species of plant and will die if they find themselves on the wrong type of tree, bush, or herb. I'm unique. My continual process of growth and what I go through determine who I am becoming. The process is unique to each one of us.

When the egg finally hatches, the caterpillar emerges. In this stage, the caterpillar eats the leaves of the plant they were born onto. As the caterpillar grows, they instantly start expanding. Their exoskeleton (skin) does not stretch, so they grow by molting. They shed their old skin several times during the growth process. As we grow, we must be careful not to consume things harmful to our growth. As we learn, we discard and let go of old habits, thoughts, and situations. We shed as much as we need during our growth process.

The pupa stage is known as the transformation stage. After the caterpillar has outgrown the last of their old skin, they form themselves into a pupa. Inside the pupa is where change rapidly occurs. Within the pupa, the old body parts of the caterpillar undergo a remarkable transformation called *metamorphosis*. This process is necessary for the creation of the beautiful parts that will emerge. My life may look like a mess, but God is doing a new thing on the inside of me. My ideas and dreams may not have manifested yet, but the work is in progress. I may still do some of the same things, but I am determined to grow and become better.

Once the caterpillar has done all its forming and changing inside the pupa, the adult emerges. In this final stage, it is written that adult butterflies are always on the lookout to reproduce, so the butterfly life cycle can start all over. They rest and mate, and new life begins. I will always look to inspire others. I will sow to produce a harvest of God's love and to reproduce in the Kingdom.

There are so many facts that were relatable; however, I'll end with this: The emergence of butterflies from the pupa typically takes place at dawn. This is when the first appearance of light comes. They begin to break open, arrive, and become evident during this time, when the darkest time meets the morning! When I read that, it began to dawn on me. While I was in the midst of trauma, challenges, and adversity, I was at the inception of a favorable time. It was the beginning, emergence, and development of a greater purpose in me—the origination of purpose inside of me. Thank you for my constant transformation. It's a butterfly thing—my process of becoming. I am hidden no more.

For You formed my inward parts;

You covered me in my mother's womb.

I will praise You, for I am fearfully *and* wonderfully made;

Marvelous are Your works,

and *that* my soul knows very well.

My frame was not hidden from You,

when I was made in secret,

and skillfully wrought in the lowest parts of the earth.

Your eyes saw my substance, being yet unformed.

And in Your book they all were written,

the days fashioned for me,

when *as yet there were* none of them.

— Psalms 139:12–16 NKJV

CHAPTER I

The Battle Within: The Woman versus the Little Girl

> When I was a child, I talked like a child, I thought
> like a child, I reasoned like a child. When I became
> a man, I put the ways of childhood behind me.
>
> —1 Corinthians 13:11 NIV

The Word said that I not only spoke and thought like a child but also that I reasoned and understood things like a child. When reading this scripture, I began to ask God what areas I still operate like a little girl in. In what areas did I need to leave the ways of the little girl I was behind me? He began to reveal how I viewed myself, friendships, men, the workplace, and even family to me and through others. Believe it or not, at the age of thirty-two, I had realized how I had emotionally operated in life as a little girl—in some ways, for years. I was stuck in an adolescent mentality.

Now some think, *oh, I'm grown.* That's fine. What is the definition of grown? They just think, *I am independent and can take care of my own.*

Our physical bodies may be grown, but our mental and spiritual states are forever growing. In order for things to grow naturally, we need to feed and cater to them. Seeds planted need watering and time to manifest. If we want to feed our minds, we read, learn, and try new things that challenge us.

A man's mind may be likened to a garden, which may be intelligently cultivated or allowed to run wild; but whether cultivated or neglected, it must, and will, bring forth. If no useful seeds are put into it, then an abundance of useless weed seeds will fall therein and will continue to produce their kind.

(Allen, 1902)

What are we doing to cultivate our minds? What seeds have been sown? Are they negative, positive, or both? What thoughts and manifestations of our characters and behaviors have come from those seeds?

To build our spirits, we pray, read the Word, and transform

our minds daily. We learn to reject our flesh and our will in substitution for God's will for our lives. We reflect on where we are versus where we want to be in every area of our lives. This is forever growing.

The Parable of the Weeds

> Jesus told them another parable: "The kingdom of heaven is like a man who sowed good seed in his field. But while everyone was sleeping, his enemy came and sowed weeds among the wheat, and went away. When the wheat sprouted and formed heads, then the weeds also appeared.
>
> "The owner's servants came to him and said, 'Sir, didn't you sow good seed in your field? Where then did the weeds come from?'
>
> "An enemy did this,' he replied.
>
> "The servants asked him, 'Do you want us to go and pull them up?'
>
> No, he answered, 'because while you are pulling the weeds, you may uproot the wheat with them. Let

both grow together until the harvest. At that time, I will tell the harvesters: First collect the weeds and tie them in bundles to be burned; then gather the wheat and bring it into my barn." (Matthew 13:24–30 NIV)

Although the parable has one true meaning explained in Matthew 13:36–40, personal revelation came. This passage blessed me as I began to read it. I imagined my life like the field. I am in the field, and as a daughter of the kingdom, seeds were sown from the beginning of my life. Seeds of purpose, prosperity, dominion, and authority. Seeds of victory, seeds of abundant life, and seeds of peace that surpass all understanding. Seeds of unconditional love, deliverance, redemption, comfort, joy, strength, endurance, and a present help.

I began to notice the tares that I had grown up with. They began to show up in my professional life, in my relationships as a mother and daughter, and in ministry. These were the areas where the enemy had used trauma, circumstances, and my choices as seeds that would grow up with what God had already placed on the inside of me. I thought of God watching the enemy and allowing some of the seeds to grow together. He knew that all the seeds the enemy had sown wouldn't destroy me. God knew that when the time came and I began to mature into what He was calling me for, He would send workers in the field of my life, and they would help me to recognize the places where the enemy had tried to destroy me by getting me to misidentify my seeds of promise.

God is exposing the enemy in this season; it's time for the removal of hurt, pain, betrayal, frustrations, anger, unforgiveness, insignificance, jealousy, impatience, low self-esteem, laziness, doubt, fear, sickness, disease, and addiction—whatever is not of the kingdom of heaven or is hindering us. As God begins to expose the areas of struggle, we take what the enemy tried to use against us—some that grew with us from childhood experiences—and we uproot them. We lay them at the altar, and we let them burn. In prayer, we release everything identified as weeds. We get up and take all the beauty that God has given us for the ashes we left.

We won't get it all at once, but every time, God allows us to identify something. We have a choice to release it and give it to God.

> Just as a gardener cultivates his plot, keeping it free
> from weeds, and growing the flowers and fruits
> which, he requires, so may a man tend the garden
> of his mind, weeding out all the wrong, useless, and
> impure thoughts, and cultivating toward perfection

the flowers and fruits of right, useful, and pure thoughts. (Allen, 1902)

If we recognize that we have yet to mature in our responses to other adults in relationships—whether personal, professional, or otherwise—or in our responses to circumstances or life's challenges, we can learn how we behave in every area of our lives. What is exemplified in our emotional responses is key to identifying and locating where we are. Is that the hurt little girl speaking or the mature woman? One still needs growth, while the other recognizes that you are constantly growing. Yes, you have been exposed to the devices of life, but it is your choice to respond to life with the maturity of knowing who you are, where you have been, and where you are purposed to go. No weapon formed shall prosper. Although the tares were sown and developed in your life, that doesn't remove the seeds of promise that were also sown.

This is our season, our harvest time. I am in the process of separating the tares from the wheat and learning how to access the harvest of promise. Will you join me? Let us continue to identify where we are and continue to mature, growing mentally and spiritually. Leave the little person behind, and move forward, into the people God has created us to become.

Heavenly Father, we are aware that we have been operating as children in some areas of our lives. Help us to identify where we are stagnant in growth. Reveal to us the areas where we still need healing and understanding. We want to grow up and fulfill our purposes so that we can assist others in their development as well. Show us how to separate the tares of our choices and life experience from the seeds influenced by the enemy who came to steal, kill, and destroy us so that we may see the promises that have been there all along. As these things are revealed, we lay them at the altar. We are putting our childish ways behind us. We are ready to embrace the next level of growth. In Jesus' name, Amen.

CHAPTER II

Reflective Perspective

A few descriptive words used for reflective are deliberation, meditative, thoughtful, contemplative. While perspective you think, viewpoint, overview, relation, context etc.

Have you ever had a moment when you were actually aware of your present thought and paused mid-thought because it was wild? Have you ever asked yourself, "Why was I thinking like that?" and were genuinely concerned? Well, I have. Most times, they were before I wanted to speak or react out of character, and I was challenged to change what I was going to say or do to reflect a more positive reaction. Before I was aware I reacted negatively— and even after—I have my moments where I reacted negatively.

It takes discipline. When we are hurt or upset, functioning with grace and positivity can be difficult. What if we take the time to reflect on why we perceive people and situations the way we do? Really think about it before we make a decision, speak our opinions, or give a piece of our mind away. Well, I need all my mind, because help, Lord.

Sorry, I digress. What if we really contemplated before we reacted the way we did, whether it be a verbal or physical altercation, like a sexual encounter or heated argument. I learned to take some time before responding, even in a text. Some things just didn't need to be said. They may have even caused damage to a healthy situation. Sometimes we must be mindful, because how we respond character or someone else's unknowingly. Taking the time to reflect on how we perceive the person or situation can be beneficial. We may find that we don't know them or are afraid, hurt, operating out of unforgiveness, or just upset. Maybe we need to take the time to calm down before we address it. So when we do react, it's the true reaction and not the impulsive one. We are still called to love and build, not tear down, especially when we are in the heat of the moment.

> Do not let any unwholesome talk come out of your
> mouths, but only what is helpful for building others

up according to their needs, that it may benefit those who listen. (Ephesians 4:29 NIV)

The word also says that we should be mindful not to pay back wrong for wrong, but always striving to do what is good for each other and for everyone else. (I Thessalonians 5:15 NIV)

This doesn't mean we won't fail. We are not perfect, and being mindful of what we say can be challenging. People will try you. Oh, do they try you! However, we should try to continuously strive for better.

Finally, brothers and sisters, whatever is true, whatever is noble, whatever is right, whatever is pure, whatever is lovely, whatever is admirable— if anything is excellent or praiseworthy—think about such things. Whatever you have learned or received or heard from me or seen in me—put it into practice. And the God of peace will be with you. (Philippians 4:8–9 NIV)

Let's practice meditating on these things, so that when faced with adverse situations, we may react the way Christ has called us to. After all, we are imitators of Him.

Heavenly Father, we are asking you to help us become more aware of how we think and why. Please forgive us for the moments of impulsive speech and behavior that were not pleasing to you. We want your perspective so that our lives may reflect an image of you. We thank you for the wisdom that is given without reproach. We desire to build one another, so we may be used to the glory of God. Teach us to put Philippians 4:8–9 into practice. We thank you. We will have mercy for others, as you have for us. We will learn patience, which will have its perfect work in us, so we will be complete, lacking nothing. In Jesus' name, Amen.

CHAPTER III

The if Factor

Facts before feeling. Allowing your mind to be led
by imaginative thoughts can lead to premature and/
or unnecessary emotions.

—LCW

What is the *if* factor? For me, it is several things:

- If I had_____, maybe he would have stayed.
- If I was enough …
- If I was different …
- If I had more money …
- If I would have chosen more wisely …

- If I could just go back …
- If they would understand …
- If I didn't love like I do …
- If I didn't make so many mistakes …
- If I had those qualities …

Some of us don't need the adversary, because we create our own thoughts of defeat.

Mostly what I find in my if challenges are my ability to see myself with certainty—the fact versus fiction. My ability to believe the fact before letting my emotions prematurely lead me down a path of doubt, fear, or frustration. The fictitious thoughts the enemy wanted me to believe versus what God said about me.

What I know is a fact is certain, it is defined, it is actual. Fiction is an imaginary, made up idea that is not certain, not true at all.

Are our thoughts proven to be true? Is there verifiable evidence that the outcome we imagine is certain? Why do we torture ourselves with if thoughts? I used to ask myself, "What if I'm not enough?" The truth is that we are created in God's image and likeness. He created us for a purpose. Before He formed us in our mothers' wombs, He said He knew us (Jeremiah 29:11). Since He is the alpha and omega, the beginning and the end, He knew that we would be blemished, not perfect, and He called us to fulfill our purpose still. What if everything you aren't, God is. It is not I but the Christ in me. I can do *all* things through Christ, who gives me strength. who is in me than he who is in the world.

(I John 4:4).

The only *if* that matters to me is this: If I didn't have Christ, where would I be? The contemplative ifs of my choices that manifest consequences also matter.

Instead of questioning, let's try believing and then doing. Then the outcome will be verifiable. If we fail, try again. If we succeed, we may possibly have the strategy for someone else's victory. Either way, it becomes a tangible experience that we can use as a point of reference, instead of an imagined outcome.

———————————————————————

Heavenly Father, sometimes we allow our minds to create scenarios, excuses, or reasons why something has or has not happened. Teach us to look at the facts and reveal the truth, so we may be able to focus on the importance of what we need to learn, not fantasize on the fictitious thoughts that create distractions from the truth. Continue to reveal our weaknesses, so we may be reminded that our strength is in you alone and continue to grow. We realize that if we have you, we are more than enough. We may not see it, but because of the great *I AM*, we can say *we are* indeed. In Jesus' name, Amen.

CHAPTER IV

Filtered Perception

> Perspective is everything. What the caterpillar calls his tomb, the butterfly calls his womb. This isn't killing you; it's birthing you!
>
> —Adrian Davis

Filtered perception is the ability to recognize and separate what is from what was and what could be. There are times when our perception—the way we see people, things, or situations—is distorted. This can affect us directly or indirectly.

Think of our minds as sieves. When we come in contact with someone or something, often there are times we don't sift or filter out the negative thoughts, opinions, biases, or even past hurts that we may have encountered. Here is a fictional example:

Sister So and So was attending Give it Up for Jesus Baptist Church, where she was treated unfairly, talked about, and intentionally hurt by some of the members. Now Sister So made mistakes, and she loved God and even apologized for her shortcomings. Still, they continued to treat her negatively, while she showed the love of God anyway. Sister So now attends the Other Side of the Pillow at her residence. Because of the hurt she experienced, she did not want to deal with church folk. One day, she went to a conference held by the local church in the neighborhood she moved into. She enjoyed the worship and the Word, so she decided to return. When the sisters began to approach her, she immediately viewed them and the things they said in a negative manner. Sister So didn't want to think negatively, as she desired fellowship; however, she was seeing through a lens of hurt and unforgiveness. Her inability to filter the past outcome to a present/future situation was affecting her.

Not all saints have a motive to hurt you. Not all men approach you with the intentions of leaving you, cheating on you, sleeping with you, or disrespecting you. Not all women are jealous or have malicious intent. This also includes how we view ourselves. We need a reflective perspective. Take time to think about why you are perceiving things in this manner and then filter the past out.

At times, our experiences cause the lenses we see out of to distort so much that we miss the purposes or possibilities of opportunities. I will share a personal example: I was in and out of a relationship for some time. Before the process of healing, God revealed how broken I had become. My self-esteem had been challenged tremendously. I was depressed. I felt defeated, and as a result, I ultimately lacked motivation to date again. I was oppressed by fear and the bondage of other people's opinions. My heart was hurt, and I felt abandoned and rejected. It seems like this is a lot for an ended relationship to cause; however, it was the assignment of the enemy to use this trial in any way that he could to demolish my character and self-worth and to distort the truth about what and why this was taking place in my life. It looked as though he had won. I sat in this state of defeat, looking out of the lens of others' opinions and feeling the manifestation of the words they intentionally and unintentionally released over me. All the while, I was feeding the spirit of people-pleasing, trying to get them to see the real me.

I developed a lens of insecurity, which caused me to make excuses for myself, him, and our situation and to explain when I didn't need to. Through the lens of victimization, I viewed things other people said I had seen as an attack against my character. For a long time, I would not give a man the time of day; I viewed through a lens of unforgiveness and a spirit of abandonment and rejection. Thank God He is the healer of broken hearts.

During the healing process, God healed my vision and heart; gave me purpose, joy, and peace; revealed unconditional love; and showed me the truth about the situation—what the enemy had wanted to happen and why I was still chosen. During that time, God did work from the inside, out every day He continues to do work. His promise to us is that He will complete the work in us that He started (Philippians 1:6).

The moment that I got rid of the why and told God I wanted to come out of where I was hiding, out of fear, and out of darkness is when things began to change. First you must ask God to show you where you are. How do you view yourself, people, circumstances, and the opposite sex? Is it the truth, or are you viewing it through a lens that God didn't intend?

One of my closest friends is a photographer. She told me about the different lenses they use in order to capture the images in the best light. Perhaps we should ask God to give us the lens of His spirit, so we may capture every person, including ourselves; every moment; and every situation that we encounter the way He sees it.

Heavenly Father, we are aware that sometimes we can perceive ourselves, people, and situations through a lens that has been distorted by our circumstances and experiences. First, we ask you to help us forgive those who have wronged us in any way, and we ask forgiveness for hurting those we may have intentionally or unintentionally wronged. In this process of forgiveness, we ask that you begin to clear our perceptions of any negative residue, so we may see ourselves, our situations, and the intentions of those we encounter through a pure lens. I thank you for teaching us to learn to filter when we should be cautious from when we are safe. I thank you for the ability to see things your way. In Jesus' name, Amen.

CHAPTER V

On the Other Side of Through

A terrible thing to see and have no vision.

—Helen Keller

For I know the plans I have for you," declares the Lord, "plans to prosper you and not to harm you, plans to give you hope and a future.

—Jeremiah 29:11 NIV

God has not forgotten you. I know sometimes it may look like it, but that's why we need to know who we are and what He has purposed for us. We need to continue to move forward and ask God to instruct us, so we may plan purposefully, especially during life's challenges. Orchestrated movement during mayhem activates our hope, builds our faith, magnetizes our answer, and manifests our purpose. The enemy comes to steal, kill, and destroy. He is after your purpose, assignment, and even those tasks you must complete during the process that leads you into your transition.

When you are going through hard times there are still decisions to be made. There are things to do. I was challenged greatly by my faith, finances, and thoughts. I found it interesting to be tempted, even by things I never struggled with and the recurrence of warfare and transgressions that I thought I had been delivered from. I began to find myself in a place of self-sabotage, and at one point, I had to stop and identify how I had gotten there. I was overwhelmed by the self-discovery, but the scariest part of it was my insensitivity to wanting to change—knowing the truth and operating as though I were ignorant while the answer was inside me. I had to come to a point where I needed to make some decisions. I knew I was at a crossroad. I was either headed to self-destruct, or I would return to my source wholeheartedly. I thought of the young ladies who called me for counsel. The women and men who approached me with their observations of my life and were inspired. I thought of my heavenly Father, who was still in pursuit of me, even in my mess. Oh, how He loves us. He gave us the greatest gift, and although we can never repay Him, we can submit ourselves and yield to His purpose and will for our lives. We can choose to give ourselves back to Him, as Jesus gave Himself for us.

These were some of my thoughts. Everything I had to endure before this moment was all a part of a purpose. It doesn't matter what we go through. How do we go through it? What are we going to do with it? Thus, the production and completion of this book. Purpose is waiting for those who choose to pursue it. We all have a purpose. Our destiny is wrapped up in our choices. Amid life happening then, you couldn't have told me that this would be my now.

> I consider that our present sufferings are not worth comparing with the glory that will be revealed in us. (Romans 8:18 NIV)

When we are going through life's challenges, we often look at our present trials and states. This, however, isn't permanent. Your present situation isn't permanent. Sometimes we are so focused on our present circumstances that we don't take time to reflect on the process; we don't take the time to celebrate the present victories or to acknowledge where we started, how far we've come, and where we are going. The enemy is a time stealer. Don't stay in longer than you have to, because God wants to bring you out, there is victory on the other side of through. Cry, but try not to go into crisis. Try to go through the process with diligence, no matter what.

> And we know that in all things God works for the good of those who love him, who have been called according to his purpose. (Romans 8:28 NIV)

Heavenly Father, we realize we will be challenged in this life. In these moments, Father, we ask you to give us continual knowledge of who we are, so we may stand firm during our trials, knowing they are temporary so we can be taught in them, and what we learn can be useful. Thank you for giving us hope and a future, so we may see past our present circumstances. Help us to identify where we are in our process and where we are fighting your will and purpose for our lives. Help us to decide to follow you wholeheartedly. We repent of all things that hinder our relationship with you. We are asking to be made in our mistakes and our present state as well as to quiet the noise, so we may hear you. Mold us to become what we need to be to fulfill purpose. Thank you for recovering all; the enemy is defeated. All will be used, nothing missing or lacking. All is for your glory, which will be revealed in us as we walk in your way. In Jesus' name, Amen.

CHAPTER VI

Detect the Decoy

We are so accustomed to disguise ourselves to others, that in the end, we become disguised to ourselves.

— François de La Rochefoucauld

Detecting is typically intentional. You are trying to find something out, it is discovery. A decoy is typically something that distracts us from the real thing. It can lead us from the original point or person intended and can sometimes be dangerous.

One day, after regretting a text conversation I'd had, I thought to myself, *why did you respond?* Then I realized that I had sent the initial text. Even though it wasn't inappropriate, it had been an introduction to the conversation. I had found out that I was being used as a decoy, so I attracted them. What happens if you detect that you are the decoy or the danger to yourself? I had realized that I was my own distraction. Believe it or not, self-sabotage can be subconscious. On several occasions, I started to realize I was the lure.

There came a time when I realized how broken I had become. I was depressed. I lacked motivation. I was afraid and hurt. My self-esteem was low. I felt defeated, and it seemed like I could not overcome the barriers I faced. Most days, it appeared as if I had it all together. My smile was a mask for the hidden tears that were flooding my insides.

I began to detect my artificial behavior. The decoy was who I portrayed versus who I believed I was. Happiness comes when the real you come out, and you see a daily manifestation of your process to become better. The good and the bad days. It was time for a reintroduction. I was done imitating the behavior of who I wanted to be and the characteristics of what I most admired. I wanted to become a person of character, not an imitator of it. Who was the woman God created me to become? I needed to become her. My pride had to bow, and as I came out of denial and exposed myself to God, He began to expose me to myself. That was when humility manifested, and my faith stood up in Him.

I began to see the areas that needed work. I continually thanked God for exposing my strengths and the areas where I am weak and need improvement. This time became my happiest moments. I had nothing and everything at the same time, because I began to learn who I was and why. Even on some of the worst days, I had joy, knowing I was being challenged to become something greater.

In the discovery of ourselves, we will find that some of the situations we find ourselves in didn't start where our emotions and hearts lead us to believe. Some traps we set ourselves. My artificial self-set me up as a decoy to accept and do things in my life that I otherwise would not have allowed.

> The discovery of you and your purpose is more powerful than the memory of you and where you were defeated.
>
> — Apostle Helen Saddler

So, what if people hold you to the last encounter? If they approach you with the same behavior, give them a new response. People cannot place you in your past if you don't allow them to. That time has gone. They must see where you are and where you are going to appreciate where you have been and how far you have come. If they can't see the hope in themselves, they won't see it in you. If you wronged them, ask for forgiveness. If they choose to hold you to the last encounter, that is their bondage, not yours. We all need forgiveness. Thank God for His grace, mercy, and love, so we may extend it to others as He has extended it to us. We cannot be the decoy in our lives, and we cannot allow the decoy to distract us. If we detect it, we can correct it.

Heavenly Father, thank you for freeing us from the snares and traps that so entangle us in our minds and even in the way we identify ourselves. Thank you for revealing the truth to us, so we may be transformed in your presence. Thank you for removing the mask in private, hiding what was ugly and exchanging it for beauty. Continue to expose every lie and every truth about who we are. We ask for discernment, so we may identify what is hindering us and luring us away from who we truly are and what our designed purpose is. In Jesus' name, Amen.

CHAPTER VII

Gambling with the Goodies

When you gamble the risk can be reckless! You are
doing something that may or may not end well. Some
people gamble with things and lose everything that
may have been extremely valuable or important.

It's interesting how, most times, we are aware of some of the
consequences of something we shouldn't do but still take the risk.
We gamble with our lives emotionally, physically, and spiritually.
We play with the call and take advantage of grace. We can play
with our relationships, professional or otherwise. We gamble with
our goodies, not just for sexual interpretation but even when we
allow ourselves to emotionally be taken to a place where our hearts

are interlocked in intimacy. When we gamble, do we see every characteristic, gift, talent, ability, or value to our time clearly? I don't believe we do. I didn't. If we did, we would not allow reckless behavior or certain situations and certain people in our lives.

So, when you gamble you run the risk of hazardous uncertainty. What are we losing when we gamble with ourselves or when we act recklessly and disregard our purpose on this earth? In a moment— in a breath—what will be lost?

In my time of self-reflection, I asked God to show me where I was gambling away my goods. It was revealed to me that I was gambling with purpose in every area of my life: in ministry, my employment, as a parent, and with illegal relationships. I placed high stakes on what came to destroy me and hinder me from obtaining God's will for my life. There is an expected end to everything.

> I make known the end from the beginning, from ancient times, what is still to come. I say, 'My purpose will stand, and I will do all that I please.' (Isaiah 46:10 NIV)

Although we may not know what the end Therefore, we should seek Him first in all things (Matthew 6:33). God has a purpose for everything. He knows our ends from our beginnings. He created us for a purpose. In all that we do, we should practice being intentional and purposeful, with something important in mind, which is who God created us to be. We must learn to practice the things of God and the principles of the kingdom of heaven. Then we have all to gain and nothing to lose, because in the process of walking with God, the Word says all things work together for our good for those who are called according to His purpose (Romans 8:28).

Notice the scripture says all things work together for our good for those who are called to *His* purpose. *His* way, not our own. We must be aware of anything that hinders us or causes us not to be victorious in this journey. Anything that causes us to gamble with His Word. Everything God placed inside of us is good. His spirit, His purpose, and anything pertaining to them are the goodies we need to protect.

Heavenly Father, we ask that you forgive us for gambling with our lives. We understand that you have placed us here for a purpose. We desire that your will be done through us on this earth. Show us where we may be behaving in a reckless manner or allowing anything that opposes your will for us. We thank you because you are making us aware of all the good things that you placed inside us. We ask that you continue to reveal not only the good things but also those things that cause us to risk losing what is most important. We now understand that your purpose stands, that you are Alpha and omega, and that you know our ends from the beginnings. Reveal to us awareness and strategy so we may see the areas that we need to improve on a day-to-day basis. Thank you for restoring all that was lost in our ignorance and for preparing us for what is to come. In Jesus' name, Amen.

CHAPTER VIII

Illegal Intimacy

"I have the right to do anything," you say—but
not everything is beneficial. "I have the right to do
anything"—but not everything is constructive.

—1 Corinthians 10:23 NIV

When we think of something illegal, we think about it
not being permitted whether by law, by social or faith/
spiritual standards, values, flagrant, not allowed. Intimacy
is a characteristic in relationships where there is familiarity,
a sense of closeness, and knowing another person.

I used to highjack moments of intimacy due to perceived moments of "loneliness." What is in a moment that will allow us to move illegally and pursue or partake in unlawful activity? This could be an activity with your friends, family, person of interest, it could be you alone.

Not all relationships are illegal; however, some have unlawful moments. What is unlawful to me may not hinder you. Anything that goes against a command from God becomes unlawful. For instance, if He asks something of us and we choose disobedience, it is illegal. Let me explain further. I would make myself available for friends when I should have been doing something else productive and purposeful. Maybe God asked me to do something in particular. Time spent with friends may have been attached to purpose or a prophetic timeline if God asked me to do it. Did I miss anything in that moment? Was it something I needed for growth or something someone else needed for survival? It may have been life altering.

I was dealing with a gentleman who I had been sexually intimate with in the past. Although I was not sexually active at the time, I was awakened when I got around him. This was because I had already experienced him. No matter how disciplined I thought I was, the truth was that it wasn't beneficial for me to spend time with him. My mind didn't benefit from the thoughts I had, and the moment my mind drifted far enough away, my body would soon follow. It quickly became an illegal situation for me to be in. Most of the time, I knew before I engaged in situations, but I just tried to reason with myself as to why I could handle it.

Instead of resisting the pressure to go into it, I succumbed to the pressure of being under it. Whether I wanted to or not, I found that an escape was always present. I had to decide to choose it. It wasn't until I became desperate for different that my indifference for righteousness became a desperation for how to attain it. Are we not content with waiting to receive what God gives us? Instead, our actions are saying that we are OK with the substitution. We are telling God that what we want right now is better.

After my last relationship, I realized that I had matured to the place of missing the person instead of missing the possibility of what we could become. I began to understand what it meant to miss the character of a person, not the possibility of being in a lasting relationship with them. Loving someone and loving the possibilities is different. Although transitioning back to being single can be challenging, I believe that my experience with him was preparing me for marriage. It taught me so much about myself and what I did and didn't desire the most. I am grateful for love's lesson. When men started to pursue me, I had a choice to be by myself or spend time with them. I began to realize that I was OK with being alone. Then the challenge of being pursued approached, and the distractions came. The Bible says it is not good for man to be alone. Men relationship; we choose to be pursued. Humans crave relationships! Although it is He who finds, we have to choose to be found. He can't find you at home, watching all the shows. Enjoy life; get out a bit!

"Wherever you discover the vacancy, fill it"

— Apostle Helen Saddler

If you know the timing is off or it isn't purposeful to pursue, fill that space with something purposeful that will enhance who you are and where you are going, not with imitators and imposters. These are the ones you aren't interested in but are just something to do. Go to eat with your friends or family, by yourself! There were times I would chill with friends, hang out with a person of interest, knowing I needed time alone. There is plenty of time for fellowship, and it is required for a healthy balanced lifestyle. However, some alone time is necessary to quiet the noise and focus.

I am an extrovert and relationship person, so naturally I have attached myself to people who I probably shouldn't have. I believe there is purpose in the exchange of a relationship professionally, spiritually, socially, and personally. There can be motive and intention. We should just know what and why it is. Some contact we have is for us to deposit and move on, and some is so we can receive or both.

In my process, I am discovering a new intimacy. This intimacy is unlike any relationship I've ever experienced. He knows me like I don't even know myself—my thoughts, every word on my tongue, and the counted hairs on my head. Every tear I cry, He catches. He formed me fearfully and wonderfully in His image. Marvelous are His works. He saw my substance and fashioned my days long before there were any. Who knows us like Him? There aren't any.

Jesus died for everything that could separate us from Him. He was beaten, bruised, and died so we could have a relationship with Him, so we could be free. He craves for us to be in a relationship with Him. This is His desire, so everything else comes secondary. Anything illegal or unlawful—the things that cause you to see yourself negatively—is what you allow to keep you from living a healthy, abundant, full life. Nothing can separate us from the love He has for us; however, our will can keep us from having a deeper relationship with Him. This process is giving me a craving—a desire to know about the One who knows all about me. This intimacy heals; releases joy, peace, and restoration; strengthens; and gives strategy and revelation. It is an intimacy that is unfailing;

loves without condition; gives mercy, grace, understanding, and wisdom; and desires you more than anyone. That intimacy is with the one who gives us instructions and clarity. He is the great comforter, the creator, and the one who is love. This love—this intimacy—is always waiting.

───────────────────────────────

Heavenly Father, we realize not all things are lawful and beneficial to us. Please help us to identify our purposes, intentions, and motives in our relationships, as well as discern the purpose of others. We want to live a healthy, balanced, abundant life. We crave relationships, because you created them. We realize the most important relationship to have is the one with you. Give us a new desire to seek after and yearn for you. Passionately, relentlessly, and with pure love, you pursue us, and with a passion to have you for real, we surrender. In Jesus' name, Amen.

CHAPTER IX

Emotional Layaway: Pursuing Potential

Ok, so growing up layaway was the move for some of us! Easter Sunday best, school clothes. The ability to shop now and pay later or over a period of time was the only way for some people to get what was needed. You get what you desire, after you have paid in full.

Sir,

I am a priority, not an option. You don't get to put me away until you are ready to sacrifice and decide to commit. You can't hold me with the emotional deposits of your charm, time, and manipulative tactics.

My time is valuable, and I do not have any to waste. You will not put me on hold, and there is no layaway option. Make a decision, whether it is to commit or not. At least show up consistently! If you want to get to know me in a more intimate, serious manner, please put in more effort.

Sincerely,

Queen

I must have had layaway option stamped on my forehead, because for a time, I attracted men who seemed to think it was OK to pursue me in intervals of their own time. Granted I participated in these attempts by allowing them, and it became apparent that I allowed them only because I was pursuing the potential of what we could become. The funny thing about becoming is that you must have consistency for it to manifest. They were not consistent in their pursuit.

Once I realized what was going on, I had to decide—allow it, continue to play the back-and-forth, or wait for a man who was willing to pursue me whole heartedly with purpose and the intention to be something more than friends if those feelings were mutual. It was a choice. I could never be upset with the men who weren't ready to commit. That was their journey and process. I was upset with myself for attaching to them. Their journey will only become a part for me to access when they include me as a permanent fixture in it. The movement of a man who is ready is strategic and thought-out. His choices include you.

What are we allowing? Why do we hold onto expectations of what could be, instead of taking hold of the reality of what is? If he is saying or showing you that he isn't ready, believe the man. Why do we sit on the emotional roller coaster and then get mad at him when we get sick and tired of riding? He gave the benediction. He didn't force us to get on. We made that choice. He showed us that he wasn't ready. We saw the potential of what we could be, so we made the choice to stay and then felt unwanted. We got upset when he still wasn't committed. It wasn't personal to him. He may have cared about you.

What would happen if we waited for men to pursue us properly in their own timing? We would go about pursuing our own desires. Are we afraid of losing out on an opportunity or being alone? What if I said that our imaginations can create the opportunities, we thought we had anyway? What type of relationship is it when only one person commits to the possibility? Potential is just an opportunity to produce or pursue something; it's the manifestation of that which had potential maturing into something productive.

Relationships only have the potential to become more if both parties are pursuing it. I would see the potential in myself or in a man. I would even take the verbal and imagined aspirations and visualize the finished state, seeing them in full operation. Realistically, this man may have never attempted to put in the effort to reach what I saw. I was a potential chaser. I had the potential to become an author. It wasn't until I started writing that it began to manifest into what you are now reading. It became productive, and God made provision for it.

Some things we must take at face value. Assess the situation and use wisdom. Take our emotions out of it and see it for what it truly is. Maya Angelou said, "If someone shows you who they are believe them." We are not creating players with qualities and characteristics that are to our expectations like my sons do in NBA2K. This is not a game. These men will become who they are meant to. They may change and become as great as we believe them to be but not in our time. Every person is different; this is my personal understanding. I have learned that sometimes you can't even remain friends; however, patience, wisdom, self-love, prayer, and the ability to stand without them in their indecision are key if you choose to be pursued again.

Father, we want to be desired, appreciated, loved, and wanted. Thank you for showing us what love truly is and giving us the wisdom to know when it isn't there. We desire to be productive in every area of our lives. Help us to cut relationships that aren't producing and to discern the intentions of those that try to attach to us. Give us the strength to carry on. We pursue you and, in our pursuit, thank you for strategically directing him. We aren't afraid of moving forward, and when presented, we thank you for making us ready to allow the right potential person to pursue us, because we know it will be productive. In Jesus' name, Amen.

CHAPTER X

Waiting without Worry

Be not impatient in delay but wait as one who understands.

—James Allen, *As a Man Thinketh*

Maybe you are waiting for a spouse, or a career change. Maybe it is a business opportunity or a response to a college application. Perhaps you desire to purchase a home, or you may be waiting for a manifestation of healing in your body. Whatever it is, James Allen says to wait as one who understands. So, while we are in the position of waiting, there an understanding that we should have? Understand what exactly?

This is the confidence we have in approaching God: that if we ask anything according to his will, he hears us. And if we know that he hears us— whatever we ask—we know that we have what we asked of him. (I John 5:14–15 NIV)

This is the confidence! We need to understand that we should have confidence in approaching God—a boldness to know that once we petition Him, He will hear us. It goes further on to say that if we are confident in knowing that He hears us, we will *know* that we will have what we asked for.

So when we worry, are we lacking confidence? Do we truly believe God will give us what we are waiting for? Do we pray with boldness and confidence, knowing that He hears us?

This doesn't mean that we won't sometimes worry or even be impatient with the process of waiting. It just means that when those moments come, we must remember what was promised, and because we understand the wait, we can become active participants in the process, instead of complainers who are filled with doubt.

In the meantime, until we see the full manifestation of what we are believing God for, remember this quote: "Let us hold unswervingly to the hope we profess, for he who promised is faithful"

(Hebrew 10:23 NIV). For the matters that we know are coming

but have no control over or the scenarios that our imaginations sometimes create due to uncertainties, remember the following:

"Therefore, do not worry about tomorrow, for tomorrow will worry about itself. Each day has enough trouble of its own" (Matthew 6:34 NIV)

Focus on being successful with your measure of faith today. Know God will come through for you. I realized I was guilty of putting my trust in people. I waited on a promise from God, expecting another person to make the decision. When it is God's timing, the decision will be made, period. God will orchestrate a man's footsteps to my heart. There is no reason to worry. What God promised in His Word will not return void. The problem is that we get in the way and put our trust in the wrong place. Let go and let God. Trust that God will direct all in the way it should go. Follow His lead along the way. We often create expectations for people that lead to disappointment. People make mistakes. We can make bad choices, but God never fails.

Although it may not be seen, stand on the promises of God, for faith is confidence in what we hope for and assurance about what we do not see (Hebrews 11:1 NIV). We may not see how or when, but we are in the position of waiting, and we believe God's promises. We wait as those who understand.

Father, we thank you for your Word and for giving us an understanding in our process of waiting. Forgive us for complaining or doubting when we didn't understand. We accept the process of the wait, and we ask you to teach and guide us in it. We thank you for replacing every moment of doubt, fear, loneliness, and frustration with patience, confidence, and understanding. Thank you for perfecting us in our patience and for the work you are doing in us so that we will be able to encourage and assist one another. We will be anxious for nothing but boldly come before your throne with our petitions, seeking only the Giver. We put our trust in you and you alone. In Jesus' name, Amen.

CHAPTER XI

The Transition

I have the desire to become, and the capacity to
evolve and grow. I am the finisher, I am determined,
and I'm coming for my best self.

—LCW

Look in the mirror and tell your best self, "I'm coming for you."
From the one who had no desire to work for my victory, I had no
hustle, no drive to complete or finish. I felt like I didn't deserve
all I had received—the jobs that kept me and the people who
blessed me and enabled me. I had to transition from laziness
and complacency to diligence and determination, from a mindset
of poverty to prosperity, from hopeful to expectant, from being

unsure to certainty, from fearful to faith-filled, from thinking and trying to doing.

> Not that I have already obtained all this, or have already arrived at my goal, but I press on to take hold of that for which Christ Jesus took hold of me. Brothers and sisters, I do not consider myself yet to have taken hold of it. But one thing I do: Forgetting what is behind and straining toward what is ahead, I press on toward the goal to win the prize for which God has called me heavenward in Christ Jesus. (Philippians 3:12–14 NIV)

Life is a continual process. We are always transitioning in some area of our lives. Whether financially, spiritually, or otherwise, we are always in movement in a way that gets us nowhere, takes us backwards or moves us ahead. While you are breathing, life is steadily in transition. It never stops.

During a particular phase of my life, I realized that the transition was major, because everything pertaining to me was shifting. It's important to know who you are while in this type of transition, because it's easy to get lost during the process. I lost focus. I created pathways that I was never supposed to take. I compromised. I made choices that weren't beneficial to my growth, and when I looked at my circumstances and current position, I forgot where I was going. I needed direction. If not, I would have continued to be all over the place, and when you have an assigned purpose in life, not having direction can interfere with those you are supposed to connect with.

I was transitioning in my mind, relationship, career, ministry, and finances as well as spiritually. Even my physical body was changing. I began to feel the weight of my choices and responsibilities and the reality of my current position. We have to continually guard our hearts in the process of living. If we don't, everything we ever hoped for, believed in, and worked toward can become unclear. Those dreams can be replaced with fear, doubt, or defeat. Transition can be difficult, and if our minds are focused, we are able to stand even in the midst of the most challenging times.

> Consider it pure joy, my brothers and sisters, whenever you face trials of many kinds, because you know that the testing of your faith produces perseverance. Let perseverance finish its work so that you may be mature and complete, not lacking anything. (James 1:2–4 NIV)

Every time we move from one place to another, we should take wisdom from our experiences, whether we were right or wrong, and choose gratitude. We may need to apply what we learned. Whether it be a hurt that we are healed from or mistake we learned from, every experience becomes healing ointment, the possibility of hope, or an answer to inspire another.

Look in the mirror, and tell your best self, "I'm coming for you." Tell your confident self. Tell your whole self. Tell your prosperous self. Tell your healed self.

Tell your victorious self. I don't know about you, but I'm coming. I'm coming for completion. Even during transition, I *am* who God says I am. Fearfully and wonderfully made, He began a good work in me.

There is beauty in the moment that you realize you are no longer afraid. No longer afraid to succeed, no longer afraid to fail, or admit you don't know what to do or how to do it. No longer afraid to make mistakes on the road of destiny and purpose or to discover who you truly are. No longer afraid to see the truth about life and its challenges and then face the challenges head on. No longer afraid to confront your weaknesses and challenge yourself to change. No longer afraid to trust God for real or to admit you can't do it on your own. No longer afraid to admit you felt abandoned. No longer afraid to be patient and wait, no matter what it looks like. No longer afraid to admit you were terrified of responsibility. No longer afraid to accept the consequences of the things you cannot change and to face the consequences of the actions you created. No longer afraid of the people you thought you had to please. Who cares what they think, darling? You were always good enough.

No longer afraid to be different, uniquely created, and fashioned by the Master's hands. Every detail of your face, the tone of your voice, your complexion, your shape, the way you laugh, and how you love were designed by God. You are beautiful—a masterpiece. No one is the same as you. Darling, you were always more than enough.

The transition was my moment of release. It was the moment when I realized that nothing else mattered, and I was completely open. When I realized I wasn't afraid anymore, I cried. Such freedom. I finally felt like this transition was nearing its end—the breakout of the butterfly. Captured, cocooned, covered, and God kept me. I went in one way, and I came out another. The pain and discomfort of the transition was worth it. Some days, the fight to break out was intense, but once my wings got loose, there was no returning. It feels like a dance, and I'm just learning to fly.

For you, it can be a dream, career, marriage, school, or maybe even a ministry that you aspire to. Do you have a vision for yourself? What do you dream about? What are you passionate about? What do you see yourself doing? Are you already in operation and want to go higher? I'm here to tell you that in the midst of all you are going through, it can and will happen. Even if it looks like it will not happen for you, it can, and it will if you believe it. God is no respecter of persons. He shows no partiality. Submit yourself and your will to the giver of all things good. Delight yourself in Him, and He will give you the desires of your heart (Psalms 37:4).

Father, thank you for teaching us through our experiences. Activate our abilities to see beyond our current revelations of who we are and where we are. While we are discovering ourselves, we thank you. We realize our purpose is more powerful than the memories of our pasts and positions where we felt defeated. In discovering the core of who we are, we recognize that the enemy couldn't have stopped us then, and he can't stop us now. We grab hold of our destinies; we make the tough decisions and move forward, into abundant living. We are no longer afraid. We have the desire to become and the capacity to evolve and grow. We are the finishers. We are determined and coming for our best selves. In Jesus' name, Amen.

CHAPTER XII

Public Disclosure

Will yourself to be what God's will designed.

—LCW

When something is public it is an open situation.
When you are disclosing information, you are sharing
something that was hidden or something new.

This was where the concept of the butterfly made sense to me. We
all have processes, and we all have a purpose. We are unique by
design. What I went through, you may not have gone through.
What you have been through in life, I may not be able to handle.
I might not be able to carry the weight of it and vice versa. No

matter what it is, it can be used to the glory of God. Your pain and your experiences can empower, inspire, and help heal someone else. Who can you assist, encourage, and love through all the challenges and hurt they may have today? People need to know how we made it and how we continue to make it. What is the purpose of your pain? The experiences we go through are not always comfortable, but they are purposeful. And there is power in sharing, we are not alone.

I didn't see how some of my experiences helped me or how they were purposeful until I started to process through some of them completely. God allowed me to see how my choices and what He allowed helped to shape and mold me into who I am now and who I am continually being shaped to become. He gave me beauty for ashes. I am a beautiful transformation and manifestation of God's Love. It's a butterfly thing.

We are breaking free from everything that tried to hold us and kept us bound in a dark place. We decide to face our issues and fears and became hidden in God's presence—His unconditional love. He wrapped us up in a cocoon, so He could comfort us, protect us, and smother us in His love while showing us who we were created to become so when we broke free, they could see the beauty of our unique life experiences reflected through us from the inside out. My name is Latrice Chenee Wyatt. This is my public service announcement, disclosed. I am hidden no more.

We are forgiven. We have been redeemed, and we are free and victorious, we are more than conquerors. We are beautiful. We are healed, blessed beyond measure, intelligent, wise, and set apart. We can do all things through Christ, who gives us the strength. We are successful and have the capacity to achieve great things. Abundant and purposeful living is waiting. Freedom is waiting. The ability to forgive ourselves and others is waiting. Healing is waiting. Hope is waiting. Happiness is waiting. Love is waiting. Peace that surpasses all understanding is waiting. Joy is waiting. Life can be beautiful if we choose, even in the midst of it being challenging. Nothing is impossible with God. If you want it, go get it. Period.

────────────────────────────────

Father, we refuse to stay hidden. We come out from mediocrity, fear, frustration, unforgiveness, hopelessness, bondage, addiction, depression, low self-esteem, and every dark place that is keeping us hidden from who we need to become. We allow the light of your Word and presence as well as your love to penetrate every area of our lives. Cocoon us in your love; mold and transform us into something beautiful. You formed our most inward parts and created us fearfully and wonderfully. Our frame was not hidden from you when you made us in secret. Reveal what you created in us so that we may become. Thank you for seeing the substance *in* us when it was yet unformed. Once we learn of ourselves, teach us how to go after others and produce after your kind. You know our ends from our beginnings, and you said they were good. Marvelous are your works; our days are written and fashioned by you. From now on, our nights will shine like the day, for your Word says that even the night shall be light about us. The darkness cannot hide from you, and we cannot hide from you. Thank you for exposing us to ourselves. We are hidden no more. In Jesus' name, Amen.

I can feel a change in me.
I feel as though I am becoming what I am
not, yet what I have always been
The sky seems closer to me though today I cannot fly
and my taste buds crave the wind
In me I feel a call to something beautiful
but when I look at me I am simply me
Am I merely a dreamer, desiring something
more then what is, NO!
This is more than me, greater than I
the call to this change is so sweet that this sound I
must follow. The touch I feel from this pull is glorious;
I must let go of what I am and in this I must be
cocooned in love, I am divinely decorated with the light
of love, the destiny with-in me is brought forth.
Nourished by bread of love, I sip from its nectar and emerge.
Free to be the me, I was created to be
I stretch forth the manifestation of merciful
love gifted to me and with its beauty,
I soar.
—Charlie F. Bufford III